rose-colored glasses

emma kaye

*to everyone who has loved and supported
me in the journey to share my poetry,
thank you from the bottom of my heart*

table of contents

PART I:
the fall

he was her sun, and she - his moon.
her existence could not be seen without his,
and his light was meaningless without her darkness.

your love is the pouring rain
my heart needed
to save it from the drought it was in.
~ i will never open an umbrella again

people say love
is the most complicated thing
one can ever experience
but i think
they are wrong.
love is simple -
i become yours,
and you become mine.
and love makes us both
simultaneously stronger
and weaker
than we have ever been before.

you were the warmth
i had searched for
in all the years
of freezing cold,
frostbite,
and ice
that my heart endured.
~ *the first sparks*

somewhere along the way,
your arms became synonymous
with the feeling of home.

~ my safe place

your laughter might possibly be the purest form of happiness my heart knows.

i have stopped shaping my future around what others
imagine a "happy life" encompasses – a successful
career, a nice house, supportive friends, loving parents,
you name it.
instead, i frame my visions around you.
you, my dearest, are the only aspect of living that is a
necessity to be content.

~ only you

time seems to slow to a stop
when i am entangled with you
you seem to have that effect on me,
transforming me into a beautiful mess
of love and tranquility

you promised to love me for eternity
not when you said "i do,"
but when you held onto me
like it was your job
to never let go.

i could be in a room with every person i'd ever met, and my heart would still find yours.

i am so lucky

to have found my South magnet

when all those before you

who claimed to never leave my side,

were later revealed

to just be other Norths.

~ you never left since we joined

the idea of having a soulmate is an interesting one –
how can someone possibly fit so seamlessly with you;
how can someone possibly be able to repair what
someone else destroyed?
i suppose the answer lies within the fact that their time
with you is meant to be filled with unimaginable joy,
pain, and love. they are not meant to last long.
but what nobody tells you is that because soulmates
can complete you so easily, it is that much easier for
them to simply detach, only to never be in your life
again.
~ *you became the one missing puzzle piece*

a dandelion
in a field full of roses
who would choose it over
the deep crimson petals
that everyone ran to?
your wilting leaves
begged for someone to
spare you a glance,
to consider you for longer
than a brief moment.
you stopped clinging onto
the ounce of hope
that someone might pick you,
the silver,
instead of the field of golds
you were surrounded by.
~ *oh but darling, i would*

since when did i reshape my life

into seeing everything as

how they relate to you?

~ *you are all i see*

at this point,
my diary should just be named
"your biography"
since all that mattered to me
from the moment we met
was you
~ *my life is yours*

you,
the bright flicker
through the vast darkness
the light spilling in
at the end of the tunnel.

you are my lifeline,
the single strand of love that grounds me to reality.
every laugh,
every smile,
every promise -
only ties our red thread tighter,
only strengthens the attachment between us
through our hearts, our minds, our souls.

you,
you are proof that people are meant to find their other
half.
i guess that is what the universe meant to do
when it created soulmates.
~ *you forever*

33

you make me feel whole,
completing the other half of me
as if the empty space in my heart
that always lacked something
was meant to be occupied by you.

~ *complete*

your eyes hold the light of a thousand stars,
brightening my world
with the love of your soul.

you are my North Star,
the center of my universe.

opening your arms
as if you would not hesitate
even for a split second,
to give me the entire world.
you never fail to show me,
to remind me,
just how much
you are able to love.

no matter how i live,
no matter who i meet,
no matter where i am,
i want you.
i would choose you
in every
single
galaxy.
~ *barycentre*

nothing will ever light up my eyes the way seeing you
does.

there is something about you
that makes me weak in the knees
even when you aren't trying
you never cease to amaze me
with just how perfect
of a human you exist to be
~ *you must have fallen from the skies*

i still feel my stomach swarm with affection
when you call me yours
even after hundreds of days together,
millions of seconds together,
and infinite moments together
~ *the answer is simple. it's you*

you,
the love
of my life.
one glance at you
makes my heart flutter,
butterflies erupting
all through my body. my life
is worth living now; i have found
meaning to the world. but love will blind
us to the devastation of heartbreak.

~ *sweet rain*

PART II:

the heartbreak

he promised her
she was his craft as the artist
he promised her
she was a real-life love letter
they would prove "forever" exists
and she was too sweet to resist
he promised her
~ *a blinding dawn*

the way you changed me,

was it ever love?

the grasp you had on me, i was never free.

the way you changed me,

the existence of "i" became "we"

and we ignored the warnings from far above.

the way you changed me,

was it ever love?

~ words from the ghost of me

maybe you and me,

the moon and the stars,

just weren't made for the same galaxy.

but the thing about love is

i tore myself apart to make it work

even after i shattered my own light,

i kept going.

further,

until i was barely a flicker in the sky

all to make you happy,

all for the moon to keep glowing.

and you,

you simply walked away

to find your sun.

~ *souls of space*

you drained all the love
from my soul. i lost myself,
my ability to love.
i finally let go of
the forgiveness you begged for.
~ *numb*

my entire being fused with the earth as i watched you walk away with my heart, unable to move as the contents of it bled out. you ripped open the stitches you mended my soul with just to take back the love you gave me. and so i watched, helplessly, as you ran away without so much as a glance back in my direction... to give her your love even though she had no room to accept it.

but my heart is still yours.

you still have pieces of me with you—you use these fragments as the sunshine and water the seedling of your heart needs to grow. i am withering; i am gasping for air and struggling to breathe. i try keeping the roots of my heart alive, but my tears are far too salty to do anything but hasten the process of destroying my sense of self. blinking them away only blurs the line between my regret and grief. my world turned dark, deprived of the light you provided it with. i made the mistake of allowing you to fill my ears with the burning lies you spoke, inhaling the poisonous air of "love" you surrounded me with.

and yet, why do i still yearn so deeply for you to be completely and utterly mine once again?
~ *the darkest night of the year*

what did i do
that made you feel
the need to run away
without ever giving
a second thought
to the pieces of me
you left behind?
~ *shipwrecked*

why do you offer love when you have none to give?
why do you accept mine knowing you won't return it?
~ *give and take*

words
the mere simplicity of them
may seem worthless
but one word
held the weight of our future
and had the potential
to heal or destroy us.

she lied to him
but still he could not think
of anything besides the fact that
she was so beautiful
~ *still in love*

our love was too sweet
that my heart died
from all the pressure,
drowning in the honey
of all your lies.

when all i could see was your back as you turned away,
i heard screaming,
drowning out any other sounds near me.
dusk enveloped the shattered pieces of me
and that's when i realized
the screaming was my own heart
begging for you to come back
and fix the fragments of me.
but alas,
there i stayed
as night fell,
and you were gone.
~ *i should have known you wouldn't return*

you never tried to love me

you never tried to love m

you never tried to love

you never tried to lov

you never tried to lo

you never tried to l

you never tried to

you never tried t

you never tried

~ *so why did you pretend like you did?*

How curious it is
For my heart to love you still
Even when every inch of my mind
Shouts your name in hatred

i used to view you
as my other half
now i look at you
and see a stranger

~ *square one*

i searched for a lost love
through an eternity
down an endless path
of thorns and tragedy
only to realize
that love never existed.

what changed?
was it me? you?
or was it our realization
that we fell in love
with the ideas of each other
rather than who we really were?

we were meant to be but not to last,
like a flame that burns bright
but extinguishes itself; becoming sparks of the past.
your eyes have forever lost that light

like a flame that burns bright
we were the water that led us to our demise.
your eyes have forever lost that light;
it is easier to see your lies.

we were the water that led us to our demise,
drowning each other in tears.
it is easier to see your lies
but i would take you back instantly, holding no fears.

drowning each other in tears,
i still would not change the love we had then.
but i would take you back instantly, holding no fears
and i promise, i will never lose you again.
~ *wistful for what once was*

PART III:
the aftermath

i wish you had fought harder for us

~ *you gave up so fast*

"till death do us part"
is the final way to secure love
so how come no one ever told me
that love itself would be the death
that made us part?

love is black and white.

it can fill you with deep, dark, aching pain

but it can also leave you in the clouds, with bright joy

and bliss

the question is,

would you prefer love to be grey?

the love that is at an eternal standstill,

a flat line.

love that will never tear you apart,

but the same love that will never take you to heaven.

~ *grey love*

why is it that nobody has ever seen the perils of love
before they devoted themselves to another?

~ *no warnings before ruin*

she told him
she would stay
for the sake of them
but he should have known
that she would never be able
to forget the past
~ *he never had the chance to say goodbye*

the force of gravitational attraction is defined as "an attractive force that exists between all objects with mass." ours was too strong it became immeasurable; undefined. undefined is another way to describe the apparent love we shared – your unclear intentions, the false smiles, the way i felt so drawn to you despite the fact that you were never able to accept me.
our undefined attraction meant we were never meant to share the same space at the same time.
~ i guess that explains why we were not meant to be

for the time you loved me,
you were always selfless
the first and only time
i ever saw you as selfish
was when you left me
but perhaps
that was the most selfless act of all

~ *perspective*

is it really considered living if you are not in my life
anymore?

~ *lost without you*

how will i ever live again
in the aftermath of you?

"just trust me," you said. "i'll show you the world."
and you showed me a mirror, watching my mouth turn
upwards in a touched smile, secretly loving the clichés
of it all.

you laughed, wrapping me in the sweet words of love,
swearing to be mine until love's end. you told me i was
more than enough to keep you on this earth.

the one thing you forgot to mention was that the love
you had, including the love you once held for yourself,
would be gone in a split second, the moment the razor
touched your wrist.

we were never enough to keep both of us on this earth
at the same time
~ *if only*

the cruelest part of you leaving this world
is most definitely the fact that you were able to love me,
but never learned to love yourself.

though i'd have liked to believe
we could last for the rest of this lifetime
and infinitely many more,
the fate of us had different plans.

we were a little bit *too* perfect for each other
to last the lifetime we planned together

how do i even begin to cope with the absence of
something, someone, that i had grown accustomed to
staying by my side? how can i learn to live as only a half,
knowing the other half of me will never return to make
a whole?

~ *questions left unanswered*

Nobody warns you about the possibility of not being able to hold onto your happiness. From the start, I only had a feeble grip on us. But I was content with it because you brought me joy the way no other person has succeeded in doing. You taught me to love, you taught me selflessness, and you taught me to be free. The one thing you forgot to teach me was how to let go.

I wish someone told me how much pain your departure would cause me before I let myself fall for you.

~ and yet, i don't regret any second of us

Perhaps I was too greedy, always wishing for *more, more, more.* More drive-in movie dates, more nights spent talking on the rooftop until we saw the first rays of the sun bleed into the sky. More hugs where we seemed to melt into each other's arms, feeling the absolute highest form of contentment being in each other's company. More sweet kisses, more absent-minded rubs on the back of my hand, more hikes to the summits of mountains where it seemed like we were invincible standing that high.

But I understand now, the one thing I failed to wish for. It seems obvious now, and I spend every day in an ocean of regret for not thinking of it. *All we needed was more time.*

If someone had offered

To erase all memories of you,

Even the most gut-wrenching painful ones,

I wouldn't hesitate for a moment

Before declining.

Because to me, the loving memories

Are worth far more to keep

Than erasing the slight pain of the others.

I'd allow myself to hurt

From the sorrow of your loss,

But if it meant I can still remember

How much happier you made me,

I would refuse the offer

Over and over again.

PART IV:
the rebuild

you were the kind of bliss
that everyone wishes for
and somehow,
i had the privilege to call you mine

perhaps the greatest gift of all was you

~ *thankful*

i would be eternally yours
the silent vow i made
stayed with me
every time you took more
of my identity.
but something changed
when i began to ignore my oath,
i found that i was able
to begin rebuilding myself
piece by piece,
taking back what was mine.
~ the forgotten promise

meeting you was like taking a breath of air after being
held underwater
loving you was like going on a roller coaster blindfolded
losing you was like being told the sun would never rise
again
grieving you was like falling for ages and never hitting
the ground

i used to wish you took me with you
but i didn't comprehend your reasons for leaving me
behind
until i remembered when you told me
you wanted to be there
when i came into your life once more
~ *a whole lifetime of second chances*

sundays are for chamomile tea and rain and classic
novels,
for fountain pens on parchment.
they are for the restoration of the soul,
for the healing.
~ *little by little*

I see you in every sunset
> But instead of closing my blinds so I wouldn't
> have to see them,
> I settle down on our hill and watch as earth
> does its magic.

I feel you in the softness of warm hoodies and cozy
blankets
> But instead of stowing away the remnants of
> you in a box,
> I keep them as reminders of how much like
> home you were to me.

I hear you in the scratching of pens against paper
> But instead of leaving all my stationary
> untouched,
> I write down all my thoughts and read them to
> you.

I taste you in sweet caramel coffee
> But instead of refusing to order that again,
> I drink it every year on your birthday.

I smell you in the cinnamon and spice of autumn
> But instead of throwing out my
> pumpkin-scented candles,
> I spend time outdoors to breathe in the fall air.

i am finally waking up again
wanting to take another breath

I think I'll always miss you, no matter the time of day or however old I live to be. But even though you now live longer in my mind than you did in this world, you continue to fill my heart with the purest forms of love to exist. I'm satisfied with how I get to share my loving memories of you with those who will listen. I'm grateful for the time we had together, even though it was cut short and not nearly as many years as we had hoped.

This was only one lifetime, though. We still have the next. And the next. And the next ones after that. For now though, all I can look forward to is when I can see you again, when I can miss you when you're right next to me instead of when you're gone.

i am at peace knowing you continue to live on in my
memories and in my heart

finally,
i have reached a point where i do not feel
an aching pain in my chest
whenever someone talks about you.
now, i smile and feel my heart warm
thinking about how lucky the world was
to have you living in it

it took awhile for me to talk about you in the past
tense,
but i no longer speak with sadness;
i voice my memories with pride.

there are some nights
i miss you so much i can hardly breathe
but when i drift off into sleep,
you comfort me with your warmth
and when morning comes,
i am no longer hurting.

who says this is the end of us?
nobody gets to decide that besides you and i,
nobody gets to say when our story is complete.
only when the world runs out of paper
will the readers stop flipping our pages.

i never thought the day would come
where i am my own person once more.
but now that i am here,
it is not all too bad
~ *regrowth*

CPSIA information can be obtained
at www.ICGtesting.com
Printed in the USA
BVHW031018120822
644452BV00011B/223

9 781088 067307